Blushing

Expressions of love

in poems &

letters

COLLECTED BY
PAUL B. JA...

SCHOLAST...
New York Toronto Lon...
Mexico City New Delhi I...

ISBN 0-439-53057-1

Introduction copyright © 2004 by Paul B. Janeczko.
Compilation copyright © 2004 by Scholastic Inc.
Pages 96–98 constitute an extension of the copyright page.
All rights reserved. Published by Orchard Books, an imprint of Scholastic Inc. ORCHARD BOOKS and design are registered trademarks of Watts Publishing Group, Ltd., used under license. SCHOLASTIC and associated logos are trademarks and/or registered trademarks of Scholastic Inc.

12 11 10 9 8 7 6 5   8 9/0

Printed in the U.S.A.   23

First Scholastic paperback printing, September 2004

Text type set in 11-point Perpetua. Display type set in LT Zapfino Two.
Cover photograph © by Melanie Acevedo/ Photonica
Book design by Marijka Kostiw

PAGES XIV–1   COPYRIGHT © BY MARIO LALICH/PHOTONICA
PAGES 24–25   COPYRIGHT © 2003 BY MARC TAUSS
PAGES 44–45   COPYRIGHT © BY KAREN BEARD/PHOTONICA
PAGES 62–63   COPYRIGHT © 2001 BY MARC TAUSS
PAGES 78–79   COPYRIGHT © BY CARLES GULLUNG/PHOTONICA

for Nadine

Lovers don't finally meet somewhere.

They're in each other all along.

— RUMI

Table of Contents

II. *In Love*

III. *Alone in Love*

IV. *The End of Love*

V. *Remembering Love*

Introduction

Why do we so often turn to poetry when we're in love? I think reading love poems is like finding a true confidant, someone who has experienced what we are experiencing. This poet *understands* me, we tell ourselves. He has been here. Felt like this. She knows. Ah, yes, we think, she has loved like this. He has fretted as I have. She has felt this pain, too. And because we are so often tongue-tied when we are in love, we seek the right words from others, from those who have loved before us. We look for validation in poetry, and for confidence. And we often find it.

But, of course, love poems also speak to us. When we read them, we, too, become the confidant, and we learn as our hearts swell with the experience of that poet. We know something about him now, and perhaps more important than that, we know something about love.

I wrote my first love poems — and the ones that have come since then — because I felt that only the intensity of poetry could convey the intensity of what I was feeling, of what I had experienced. Love letters, too, are wonderful and intimate ways to communicate — as you'll see in the handful that I've used to introduce each section of poems in this collection — but they tend to be undisciplined. They have, in some instances, the feeling that they might be the first drafts of poems. But we know, if we are going to write a love poem, that the poem must show concentration of mind and heart, which means finding the best words, images, and rhythm. That poem must be the very music of love itself.

The poems in this collection are organized in a way that reflects many love affairs. The opening section is filled with poems that convey the utter excitement of first love. Nineteenth-century poet John Clare is struck "With love so sudden and so sweet" that he feels his heart "has left its dwelling-place/And can return no more." Over 125 years later, Maya Angelou writes how love "rose into my life/Like a promised sunrise."

These poems are followed by a group of poems that speak to a more mature love, a love that has had time to grow. Chilean poet Pablo Neruda loves "without knowing how, or when, or from where" it came. And Ann Bradstreet tells her husband, "I prize thy love more than whole mines of gold. . . ."

Somewhere around page 48, however, the tone of the poems changes. Gone are the cries of delight, the proclamations of mutual affection. Instead the poet is often alone in love, either separated from his love or feeling regret for allowing a moment, a love, to slip away. Juana Inés de la Cruz is caught in her love: "I can't hold you and I can't leave you," while Thomas Hardy writes of regret: "I should have kissed her if the rain/Had lasted a minute more."

The poems in the fourth section are about the end of love. Sometimes we are left bitter and tormented when love fades. Or, we feel deep sadness or loneliness at the end of love. These poems express the pain, the emptiness that comes with the end of love. Christina Rossetti, for example, speaks of such emptiness when she writes, "With all sweet things it passed away,/And left me old, and cold, and grey." On the other hand, contemporary British poet Sophie Hannah speaks with bitterness when she writes, "The end of love should be a big event./It should involve the hiring of a hall."

It is in the final section of poems that the tone changes yet again, back toward hopeful. The poems express the resilience of the human heart. Here, poets remember their loves and note how their lives have been altered by love. How they have grown and moved on. How they will love differently when love comes around again. Vickie Feaver remembers the pleasures of lost love: "I feel the cold/and all the time I think/how warm it used to be." Hungarian poet Miklos Radnoti dreams of his lost love: "I often have a hundred arms/and like god in a dream/I hold you in those arms."

When I set out to collect love poems for this volume, I knew one thing for certain: I didn't want to include only poems about the glories of new love, because love gets complicated. It is exciting when it begins, but it can also be exciting when it grows deeper, and confusing when it is no more. So I looked for longing, too, and for heartbreak — and I found so much more. Poems that speak of the shades of love.

I looked also for poems that show how love spans the ages. It is classic and modern at once. Love is in the poems of Lord Byron and Robert Creeley. It is in the poems of William Shakespeare and Maya Angelou. And it is in the sonnets of Elizabeth Barrett Browning and Edna St. Vincent Millay.

I hope that these poems will speak to you as they have spoken to me. I hope that you will return to them when love changes for you, when you need solace or encouragement. Because beyond that first blush, the pink that colors your cheeks when you realize that something in someone has changed you, you will find that love gets messy and real.

The Beginning of Love

Sunday night

August 25, 1928

Francis darling,

Have you heard that I love you? I'm not sure that I made it clear to you, and I don't want to have any misunderstanding. It's such a young love yet — just nine and a half months old, born November 13th 1928 at about nine o'clock in the evening. But it's big for its age, and seems much older. I do hope you're going to like it, I'm sending you some now for you to try; but I don't want to. I've wanted to try it out for a long time; I like the look of it and the sound of it and the meaning of it.

It's past one now and I've got to get some sleep before [my meeting with a publisher] tomorrow. But tell me something before I leave. I was told tonight on what seemed to me the best authority that you are fond of me. Can you confirm this rumor.

Then there's another problem. As long as I'm thinking about you I can't go to sleep; and I'd rather think about you than to go sleep; how am I to sleep?

Oh Frances, do tell me that everything really happened, that it wasn't just something that I wanted so much that it crystalized in my imagination.

Good night. I've just sent St. Joseph off to watch you on the train; he has promised that he will do his duty like an honest saint.

I do love you.

Ogden

First Love

JOHN CLARE

I ne'er was struck before that hour
With love so sudden and so sweet,
Her face it bloomed like a sweet flower
And stole my heart away complete.
My face turned pale as deadly pale.
My legs refused to walk away,
And when she looked, what could I ail?
My life and all seemed turned to clay.

And then my blood rushed to my face
And took my eyesight quite away,
The trees and bushes round the place
Seemed midnight at noonday.
I could not see a single thing,
Words from my eyes did start —

They spoke as chords do from the string,
And blood burnt round my heart.

Are flowers the winter's choice?
Is love's bed always snow?
She seemed to hear my silent voice,
Not love's appeals to know.
I never saw so sweet a face
As that I stood before.
My heart has left its dwelling-place
And can return no more.

She Was a Phantom of Delight

WILLIAM WORDSWORTH

She was a Phantom of delight
When first she gleamed upon my sight;
A lovely Apparition, sent
To be a moment's ornament;
Her eyes as stars of Twilight fair;
Like Twilight's, too, her dusky hair;
But all things else about her drawn
From May-time and the cheerful Dawn;
A dancing Shape, an Image gay,
To haunt, to startle, and way-lay.

I saw her upon nearer view,
A Spirit, yet a Woman too!
Her household motions light and free,
And steps of virgin-liberty;
A countenance in which did meet

Sweet records, promises as sweet;
A Creature not too bright or good
For human nature's daily food;
For transient sorrows, simple wiles,
Praise, blame, love, kisses, tears, and smiles.

And now I see with eye serene
The very pulse of the machine;
A Being breathing thoughtful breath,
A Traveler between life and death;
The reason firm, the temperate will,
Endurance, foresight, strength, and skill;
A perfect Woman, nobly planned,
To warn, to comfort, and command;
And yet a Spirit still, and bright
With something of angelic light.

THE BEGINNING OF LOVE

To Citriodora

PHILIP HENRY SAVAGE

I turn and see you passing in the street
When you are not. I take another way,
Lest missing you the fragrance of the day
Exhale, and I know not that it is sweet.
And marking you I follow, and when we meet
Love laughs to see how sudden I am gay;
Sweetens the air with fragrance like a spray
Of sweet verbena, and bids my heart to beat.

Love laughs; and girls that take you by the hand,
Know that a sweet thing has befallen them;
And women give their hearts into your heart.
There is, I think, no man in all the land
But would be glad to touch your garment's hem.
And I, I love you with a love apart.

Shall I Compare Thee to a Summer's Day?

WILLIAM SHAKESPEARE

Shall I compare thee to a summer's day?
Thou art more lovely and more temperate:
Rough winds do shake the darling buds of May,
And summer's lease hath all too short a date:
Sometime too hot the eye of heaven shines,
And often is his gold complexion dimm'd;
And every fair from fair sometime declines,
By chance, or nature's changing course, untrimm'd;
But thy eternal summer shall not fade,
Nor lose possession of that fair thou owest;
Nor shall Death brag thou wander'st in his shade,
When in eternal lines to time thou growest;

    So long as men can breathe, or eyes can see,
    So long lives this, and this gives life to thee.

She Walks in Beauty

LORD BYRON

She walks in beauty, like the night
Of cloudless climes and starry skies;
And all that's best of dark and bright
Meet in her aspect and her eyes:
Thus mellow'd to that tender light
Which heaven to gaudy day denies.

One shade the more, one ray the less,
Had half impair'd the nameless grace
Which waves in every raven tress,
Or softly lightens o'er her face;
Where thoughts serenely sweet express
How pure, how dear their dwelling-place.

And on that cheek, and o'er that brow,
So soft, so calm, yet eloquent,
The smiles that win, the tints that glow,
But tell of days in goodness spent,
A mind at peace with all below,
A heart whose love is innocent!

Feste's Song (from Twelfth Night)

WILLIAM SHAKESPEARE

O mistress mine, where are you roaming?
O! stay and hear; your true love's coming,
    That can sing both high and low.
Trip no further, pretty sweeting;
Journeys end in lovers meeting,
    Every wise man's son doth know.

What is love? 'Tis not hereafter;
Present mirth hath present laughter;
    What's to come is still unsure.
In delay there lies no plenty;
Then come kiss me, sweet and twenty;
    Youth's a stuff will not endure.

To Celia

BEN JONSON

Drink to me only with thine eyes,
 And I will pledge with mine;
Or leave a kiss but in the cup
 And I'll not look for wine.
The thirst that from the soul doth rise
 Doth ask a drink divine;
But might I of Jove's nectar sup,
 I would not change for thine.

I sent thee late a rosy wreath,
 Not so much honouring thee
As giving it a hope that there
 It could not wither'd be;
But thou thereon didst only breathe,
 And sent'st it back to me;
Since when it grows, and smells, I swear,
 Not of itself but thee!

An Hour with Thee

SIR WALTER SCOTT

An hour with thee! When earliest day
Dapples with gold the eastern grey,
Oh, what can frame my mind to bear
The toil and turmoil, cark and care,
New griefs, which coming hours unfold,
And sad remembrance of the old?
One hour with thee.

One hour with thee! When burning June
Waves his red flag at pitch of noon;
What shall repay the faithful swain,
His labour on the sultry plain;
And, more than cave or sheltering bough,
Cool feverish blood and throbbing brow?
One hour with thee.

One hour with thee! When sun is set,

Oh, what can teach me to forget

The thankless labours of the day;

The hopes, the wishes, flung away;

The increasing wants, and lessening gains,

The master's pride, who scorns my pains?

One hour with thee.

I Shall Hide Myself

CHINO MASAKO

> I shall hide myself
>
> within the moon of the spring night,
>
> after I have dared to reveal
>
> my love to you.

She Tells Her Love While Half Asleep

ROBERT GRAVES

> She tells her love while half asleep
>   In the dark hours,
>   With half-words whispered low:
> As Earth stirs in her winter sleep
>   And puts out grass and flowers
>   Despite the snow,
>   Despite the falling snow.

Love Comes Quietly

ROBERT CREELEY

Love comes quietly,
finally, drops
about me, on me
in the old ways.

What did I know
thinking myself
able to go
alone all the way.

Kidnap Poem

NIKKI GIOVANNI

ever been kidnapped

by a poet

if i were a poet

i'd kidnap you

put you in my phrases and meter

you to jones beach

or maybe coney island

or maybe just to my house

lyric you in lilacs

dash you into the beach

to complement my see

play the lyre for you

ode you with my love song

anything to win you

wrap you in the red Black green

show you off to mama

yeah if i were a poet i'd kid

nap you

Where We Belong, A Duet

MAYA ANGELOU

In every town and village,
In every city square,
In crowded places
I search the faces
Hoping to find
Someone to care.

I read mysterious meanings
In the distant stars,
Then I went to schoolrooms
And poolrooms
And half-lighted cocktail bars.
Braving dangers,
Going with strangers,
I don't even remember their names.
I was quick and breezy
And always easy
Playing romantic games.

I wined and dined a thousand exotic Joans and

Janes

In dusty dance halls, at debutante balls,

On lonely country lanes.

I fell in love forever,

Twice every year or so.

I wooed them sweetly, was theirs completely,

But they always let me go.

Saying bye now, no need to try now,

You don't have the proper charms.

Too sentimental and much too gentle

I don't tremble in your arms.

Then you rose into my life

Like a promised sunrise.

Brightening my days with the light in your eyes.

I've never been so strong.

Now I'm where I belong.

First Time He Kissed Me, He but Only Kissed

ELIZABETH BARRETT BROWNING

First time he kissed me, he but only kiss'd

The fingers of this hand wherewith I write;

And ever since, it grew more clean and white,

Slow to world-greetings, quick with its "Oh, list,"

When the angels speak. A ring of amethyst

I could not wear here, plainer to my sight,

Than that first kiss. The second pass'd in height

The first, and sought the forehead, and half miss'd,

Half falling on the hair. Oh, beyond meed!

That was the chrism of love, which love's own crown,

With sanctifying sweetness, did precede.

The third upon my lips was folded down

In perfect, purple state; since when, indeed,

I have been proud, and said, "My love, my own!"

In Your Light I Learn How to Love

RUMI

In your light I learn how to love.
In your beauty, how to make poems.

You dance inside my chest,
where no one sees you,

but sometimes I do,
and that sight becomes this art.

In Love

March 1820

Sweetest Fanny,

You fear, sometimes, I do not love you so much as you wish? My dear Girl I love you ever and ever and without reserve. The more I have known you the more have I lov'd. In every way — even my jealousies have been agonies of Love, in the hottest fit I ever had I would have died for you. I have vex'd you too much. But for Love! Can I help it? You are always new. The last of your kisses was ever the sweetest; the last smile the brightest; the last movement the gracefullest. When you pass'd my window home yesterday, I was fill'd with as much admiration as if I had then seen you for the first time. You uttered a half complaint once that I only lov'd your Beauty. Have I nothing else then to love in you but that: Do not I see a heart naturally furnish'd with wings imprison itself with me? No ill prospect has been able to turn your thoughts a moment from me. This perhaps should be as much a subject of sorrow as joy — but I will not talk of that. Even if you did not love me I could not help an entire devotion to you: How much more deeply then must I feel for you knowing you love me. My Mind has been the most discontented and restless one that ever was put into a body too small for it. I never felt my Mind repose upon anything with complete and undistracted enjoyment — upon no person but you. When you are in the room my thoughts never fly out the window: you always concentrate my whole senses. The anxiety shown about our Loves in your last note is an immense pleasure to me: however you must not suffer such speculations to molest you any more: nor will I any more believe you can have the least pique against me. Brown is gone out — but here is Mrs. Wylie — when she is gone I will be awake for you.

Your affectionate

J. Keats

Deep in Love

BHAVABHŪTI

Deep in love

cheek leaning on cheek we talked

of whatever came to our minds

just as it came

slowly oh

slowly

with our arms twined

tightly around us

and the hours passed and we

did not know it

still talking when

the night had gone

To My Dear and Loving Husband

ANNE BRADSTREET

If ever two were one, then surely we.

If ever man were loved by wife, then thee;

If ever wife was happy in a man,

Compare with me, ye women, if you can.

I prize thy love more than whole mines of gold,

Or all the riches that the East doth hold.

My love is such that rivers cannot quench,

Nor aught but love from thee, give recompense.

Thy love is such I can no way repay,

The heavens reward thee manifold, I pray.

Then while we live, in love let's so persever

That when we live no more, we may live ever.

The Passionate Shepherd to His Love

CHRISTOPHER MARLOWE

Come live with me and be my Love,
And we will all the pleasures prove
That hills and valleys, dales and fields,
Or woods or steepy mountain yields.

And we will sit upon the rocks,
And see the shepherds feed their flocks
By shallow rivers, to whose falls
Melodious birds sing madrigals.

And I will make thee beds of roses
And a thousand fragrant posies;
A cap of flowers, and a kirtle
Embroider'd all with leaves of myrtle.

A gown made of the finest wool
Which from our pretty lambs we pull;
Fair-lined slippers for the cold,
With buckles of the purest gold.

A belt of straw and ivy-buds
With coral clasps and amber studs:
And if these pleasures may thee move,
Come live with me and be my Love.

The shepherd swains shall dance and sing
For thy delight each May morning:
If these delights thy mind may move,
Then live with me and be my Love.

The Good-Morrow

JOHN DONNE

I wonder, by my troth, what thou and I
Did, till we loved? were we not weaned till then?
But sucked on country pleasures, childishly?
Or snorted we in the Seven Sleepers' den?
'Twas so; but this, all pleasures fancies be.
If ever any beauty I did see,
Which I desired, and got, 'twas but a dream of thee.

And now good-morrow to our waking souls,
Which watch not one another out of fear;
For love, all love of other sights controls,
And makes one little room an everywhere.
Let sea-discoverers to new worlds have gone,
Let maps to others, worlds on worlds have shown,
Let us possess one world, each hath one, and is one.

My face in thine eye, thine in mine appears,

And true plain hearts do in the faces rest;

Where can we find two better hemispheres,

Without sharp North, without declining West?

Whatever dies was not mixed equally;

If our two loves be one, or, thou and I

Love so alike that none do slacken, none can die.

How Do I Love Thee? Let Me Count the Ways

ELIZABETH BARRETT BROWNING

How do I love thee? Let me count the ways.
I love thee to the depth and breadth and height
My soul can reach, when feeling out of sight
For the ends of Being and ideal Grace.
I love thee to the level of everyday's
Most quiet need, by sun and candle-light.
I love thee freely, as men strive for Right;
I love thee purely, as they turn from Praise.
I love thee with the passion put to use
In my old griefs, and with my childhood's faith.
I love thee with a love I seemed to lose
With my lost saints, — I love with the breath,
Smiles, tears, of all my life! — and, if God choose,
I shall but love thee better after death.

i carry your heart with me (i carry it in

e . e . c u m m i n g s

i carry your heart with me(i carry it in
my heart)i am never without it(anywhere
i go you go,my dear; and whatever is done
by only me is your doing,my darling)

                                i fear

no fate(for you are my fate,my sweet)i want
no world(for beautiful you are my world,my true)
and it's you are whatever a moon has always meant
and whatever a sun will always sing is you

here is the deepest secret nobody knows
(here is the root of the root and the bud of the bud
and the sky of the sky of a tree called life;which grows
higher than the soul can hope or mind can hide)
and this is the wonder that's keeping the stars apart

i carry your heart(i carry it in my heart)

A Sonnet of the Moon

CHARLES BEST

Look how the pale queen of the silent night
Doth cause the ocean to attend upon her,
And he, as long as she is in his sight,
With her full tide is ready her to honor.
But when the silver waggon of the moon
Is mounted up so high he cannot follow,
The sea calls home his crystal waves to moan,
And with low ebb doth manifest his sorrow.
So you that are the sovereign of my heart
Have all my joys attending on your will;
My joys low-ebbing when you do depart,
When you return their tide my heart doth fill.
So as you come and as you do depart,
Joys ebb and flow within my tender heart.

Warmth

BARTON SUTTER

Sometimes want makes touch too much.
I hold my hands over your body
Like someone come in from the cold
Who takes off his clothes
And holds out his hands to the stove.

I Do Not Love You . . .

PABLO NERUDA

I do not love you as if you were salt-rose, or topaz,

or the arrow of carnations the fire shoots off.

I love you as certain dark things are to be loved,

in secret, between the shadow and the soul.

I love you as the plant that never blooms

but carries in itself the light of hidden flowers;

thanks to your love a certain solid fragrance,

risen from the earth, lives darkly in my body.

I love you without knowing how, or when, or from where.

I love you straightforwardly, without complexities or

   pride;

so I love you because I know no other way

than this: where I does not exist, nor you,

so close that your hand on my chest is my hand,

so close that your eyes close as I fall asleep.

Roadmap —for J.R.

HARRYETTE MULLEN

She wants a man she can just
unfold when she needs him
then fold him up again
like those 50 cent raincoats
women carry in their purses
in case they get caught in stormy weather.

This one has her thumb out
for a man who's going her way.
She'll hitch with him awhile,
let him take her down the road
for a piece.

But I want to take you where you're going.
I'm unfolding for you
like a roadmap you can never again fold up
exactly the same as before.

Loving Again

GLORIA WADE-GAYLES

Last night
we loved as if the gods
had announced only to us
that the sky would fall
while we slept.

We loved
passionately
selflessly
thinking only of pleasure
giving pleasure,

and I knew I would not grieve
if life should end as you held me.

Daybreak.

The sun slid silently
into our room
kissed our faces
and lay softly
in our love bed.

The sky had not fallen.

The earth had not disappeared.

We were alive
to love again.

I Want to Die While You Love Me

GEORGIA DOUGLAS JOHNSON

I want to die while you love me,
While yet you hold me fair,
While laughter lies upon my lips
And lights are in my hair.

I want to die while you love me
And bear to that still bed
Your kisses turbulent, unspent
To warm me when I'm dead.

I want to die while you love me

    Oh, who would care to live

Till love has nothing more to ask

    And nothing more to give?

I want to die while you love me

    And never, never see

The glory of this perfect day

    Grow dim or cease to be!

Alone in
Love

September 6th 1910

. . . At that point, I went & had tea. And now, do you know, I feel quite cheerful again. That's the worst of writing letters. They only give the writer as he is during a certain hour; not the writer as he is during a month or a year: nor, possibly, just — the writer. I might easily write during a time when I didn't care twopence whether you lived or died or what you did, & convey a false impression that I'd fallen quite out of love with you, and so (conceivably) relieve, or irritate you — unnecessarily. Or, what'd be even, perhaps, tiresomer, I might write during one of the horrible periods when I realize that unless I'm thinking of you every minute, and unless I'm Tristan-drunk all the time, I'm not being fine enough for you, not treating you worthily.

But, just now, — and pretty often — I'm immensely cheery. I go bounding through life. "Do not" I say to the parlormaid "look at me as if I was a Common Person. I am not. I am Unique; Marked out above all men. I will explain." And I dance to her the reason. Yesterday I stopped before the fat policeman at the corner. "You look as if you thought you were Important;" I told him, "Know then that I barely realise your existence. I soar above you. — Ah, but you've never met Noel, eh, Old Thing?"

I've a million things to discuss tell, & ask. That's partly when I must see you, sometime. I've never had time to mention you half the things I wanted to spend hours in explaining. If ever we do meet again, we might make a rule that we are to spend at least two hours in rational conversation every time we're together. It'd be good for our characters anyhow!

Yes, dammit, I *am* glad you're existing away from me among & for other people; just that you're existing, quite glad, quite fairly glad.

I do want to see you. But don't reckon that. I'm very happy.

It's *very* queer, this should be <u>me</u> writing to <u>you</u> —

How do I end up this? I'm afraid. I shall just write my name —

Rupert

Oh, I want to go *on* writing, so!

N o - e l !

Separation

W .   S .   M E R W I N

Your absence has gone through me

Like thread through a needle

Everything I do is stitched with its color.

A Thunderstorm in Town (A Reminiscence: 1893)

THOMAS HARDY

She wore a new 'terra-cotta' dress,
And we stayed, because of the pelting storm,
Within the hansom's dry recess,
Though the horse had stopped; yea, motionless
    We sat on, snug and warm.

Then the downpour ceased, to my sharp sad pain,
And the glass that had screened our forms before
Flew up, and out she sprang to her door:
I should have kissed her if the rain
    Had lasted a minute more.

Song

J O H N   C L A R E

I hid my love when young while I
Couldn't bear the buzzing of a fly
I hid my love to my despite
Till I could not bear to look at light
I dare not gaze upon her face
But left her memory in each place
Where e're I saw a wild flower lie
I kissed and bade my love good bye

I met her in the greenest dells
Where dew drops pearl the wood blue bells
The lost breeze kissed her bright blue eye
The Bee kissed and went singing by
A sun beam found a passage there
A gold chain round her neck so fair

As secret as the wild bees' song
She lay there all the summer long

I hid my love in field and town
Till e'en the breeze would knock me down
The Bees seemed singing ballads o'er
The flys' buzz turned a Lion's roar
And even silence found a tongue
To haunt me all the summer long
The Riddle nature could not prove
Was nothing else but secret love

Rondeau

JAMES HENRY LEIGH HUNT

Jenny kissed me when we met,
    Jumping from the chair she sat in;
Time, you thief, who love to get
    Sweets into your list, put that in:

Say I'm weary, say I'm sad,
    Say that health and wealth have missed me,
Say I'm growing old, but add,
    Jenny kissed me.

S A R A   T E A S D A L E

Strephon kissed me in the spring,
    Robin in the fall,
But Colin only looked at me
    And never kissed at all.

Strephon's kiss was lost in jest,
    Robin's lost in play,
But the kiss in Colin's eyes
    Haunts me night and day.

Nineteen

GEORGE BOGIN

On the first day of Philosophy 148, a small girl walked in,
freckled, solemn, cute, whom I liked right off.

Next time, our eyes met and she smiled a little.
I was already in love.

I always tried to arrive before she did so I could watch her
coming through the doorway, each time loving her more.

She began to look at me, too, hoping for a word, I suppose,
but when our eyes met mine would drop.

Once I heard her ask someone for a pencil.
I passed mine back without turning or speaking.

Spring came and we saw each other on the campus
open-throated, wordless, everywhere.

On the last day of exam week I was reading at the far end
of the Philosophy Library. Not a soul there but the librarian.
Dust in the sunbeams. End of college.

The door opened. It was my girl. I looked down.

In all that empty library she came to my side,
to the very next chair. Sweet springtime love.
Lovely last chance first love.

I could have taken her by the hand and walked the whole
        60 blocks
to the piers right onto a steamer to France or somewhere,
but I said nothing and after a while got up
and walked out into middle age.

I Think I Should Have Loved You Presently

EDNA ST. VINCENT MILLAY

I think I should have loved you presently,

And given in earnest words I flung in jest;

And lifted honest eyes for you to see,

And caught your hand against my cheek and breast;

And all my pretty follies flung aside

That won you to me, and beneath your gaze,

Naked of reticence and shorn of pride,

Spread like a chart my little wicked ways.

I, that had been to you, had you remained,

But one more waking from a recurrent dream,

Cherish no less the certain stakes I gained,

And walk your memory's halls, austere, supreme,

A ghost in marble of a girl you knew

Who would have loved you in a day or two.

The Taxi

AMY LOWELL

When I go away from you

The world beats dead

Like a slackened drum.

I call out for you against the jutted stars

And shout into the ridges of the wind.

Streets coming fast,

One after the other,

Wedge you away from me,

And the lamps of the city prick my eyes

So that I can no longer see your face.

Why should I leave you,

To wound myself upon the sharp edges of the night?

Everybody Tells Me

L A D Y   S O N O   N O   O M I   I K U H A

Everybody tells me

My hair is too long

I leave it

As you saw it last

Dishevelled by your hands.

Waiting

YEVGENY YEVTUSHENKO

My love will come

will fling open her arms and fold me in them,

will understand my fears, observe my changes.

In from the pouring dark, from the pitch night

without stopping to bang the taxi door

she'll run upstairs through the decaying porch

burning with love and love's happiness,

she'll run dripping upstairs, she won't knock,

will take my head in her hands,

and when she drops her overcoat on a chair,

it will slide to the floor in a blue heap.

I Can't Hold You and I Can't Leave You

JUANA INÉS DE LA CRUZ

I can't hold you and I can't leave you,
and sorting the reasons to leave you or hold you,
I find an intangible one to love you,
and many tangible ones to forgo you.

As you won't change, nor let me forgo you,
I shall give my heart a defence against you,
so that half shall always be armed to abhor you,
though the other half be ready to adore you.

Then, if our love, by loving flourish,
let it not in endless feuding perish;
let us speak no more in jealousy and suspicion.

He offers not part, who would all receive —
so know that when it is your intention
mine shall be to make believe.

Dream

LANGSTON HUGHES

Last night I dreamt
This most strange dream,
And everywhere I saw
What did not seem could ever be:

You were not there with me!

Awake,
I turned
And touched you
Asleep,
Face to the wall.

I said,
How dreams
Can lie!

But you were not there at all!

The End of Love
of Love

London, October 3, 1814

I am united to another; you are no longer my wife. Perhaps I have done you injury, but surely most innocently & unintentionally in having commenced any connexion with you. — That injury whatever be its amount was not to be avoided. If ever in any degree there was sympathy in our feelings & opinions wherefore deprive ourselves in future of the satisfaction which may result, by this contemptible cavil — these unworthy bickerings. Unless a sincere confidence be accorded by you to my undesigning truth, our intercourse for the present must be discontinued. You derive more pain that advantage from irritations produced by my visits. The interest which I take in you is disturbed by no feelings which prevent me from calmly calculating on your happiness.

Collect yourself I entreat you: remember what I am: recall your recollections of my character. The hint respecting my duty to settle the property on you which your letter contains proves how little you can appreciate it. — You have little need to fear that I shall fail in real duty.

Affectionately your

P. B. Shelley

I hope that you will attend to the preservation of your health: I do not apprehend the slightest danger from your approaching labour: I think you may safely repose confidence in [your physician's] skill. Your last labour was painful, but auspicious. I understand that cases of difficulty after that are very rare.

My dear Harriet, I am anxious for your answer, you must not do me injustice you have done so I expect you to repair it. I see Hookham tonight. I am in want of stockings, hanks & Mrs. W[ollstonecrafts]'s posthumous works.

The End of Love

SOPHIE HANNAH

The end of love should be a big event.
It should involve the hiring of a hall.
Why the hell not? It happens to us all.
Why should it pass without acknowledgement?

Suits should be dry-cleaned, invitations sent.
Whatever form it takes — a tiff, a brawl —
The end of love should be a big event.
It should involve the hiring of a hall.

Better than the unquestioning descent
Into the trap of silence, than the crawl
From visible to hidden, door to wall.

Get the announcement made, the money spent.
The end of love should be a big event.
It should involve the hiring of a hall.

Like the Touch of Rain

EDWARD THOMAS

Like the touch of rain she was
On a man's flesh and hair and eyes
When the joy of walking thus
Has taken him by surprise:

With the love of the storm he burns,
He sings, he laughs, well I know how,
But forgets when he returns
As I shall not forget her "Go now."

Those two words shut a door
Between me and the blessed rain
That was never shut before
And will not open again.

Neutral Tones

THOMAS HARDY

We stood by a pond that winter day,
And the sun was white, as though chidden of God,
And a few leaves lay on the starving sod;
— They had fallen from an ash, and were gray.

Your eyes on me were as eyes that rove
Over tedious riddles of years ago;
And some words played between us to and fro
On which lost the more by our love.

The smile on your mouth was the deadest thing
Alive enough to have strength to die;
And a grin of bitterness swept thereby
    Like an ominous bird a-wing. . . .

Since then, keen lessons that love deceives,
And wrings with wrong, have shaped to me
Your face, and the God-curst sun, and a tree,
    And a pond edged with grayish leaves.

May

CHRISTINA ROSETTI

I cannot tell you how it was;
But this I know: it came to pass —
Upon a bright and breezy day
When May was young, ah pleasant May!
As yet the poppies were not born
Between the blades of tender corn;
The last eggs had not hatched as yet,
Nor any bird forgone its mate.

I cannot tell you what it was;
But this I know: it did but pass.
It passed away with sunny May,
With all sweet things it passed away,
And left me old, and cold, and grey.

Heart! We Will Forget Him

EMILY DICKINSON

Heart! We will forget him!
You and I — tonight!
You may forget the warmth he gave —
I will forget the light!

When you have done, pray tell me
That I may straight begin!
Haste! lest while you're lagging
I remember him!

Time Does Not Bring Relief

EDNA ST. VINCENT MILLAY

Time does not bring relief; you all have lied
Who told me time would ease me of my pain!
I miss him in the weeping of the rain;
I want him at the shrinking of the tide;
The old snows melt from every mountain-side,
And last year's leaves are smoke in every lane;
But last year's bitter loving must remain
Heaped on my heart, and my old thoughts abide.
There are a hundred places where I fear
To go, — so with his memory they brim.
And entering with relief some quiet place
Where never fell his foot or shone his face
I say, "There is no memory of him here!"
And so stand stricken, so remembering him.

Never Again Would Birds' Song Be the Same

ROBERT FROST

He would declare and could himself believe
That the birds there in all the garden round
From having heard the daylong voice of Eve
Had added to their own an oversound,
Her tone of meaning but without the words.
Admittedly an eloquence so soft
Could only have had an influence on birds
When call or laughter carried it aloft.
Be that as may be, she was in their song.
Moreover her voice upon their voices crossed
Had now persisted in the woods so long
That probably it never would be lost.
Never again would birds' song be the same.
And to do that to birds was why she came.

When I Was One-and-Twenty
(from A Shropshire Lad)

A. E. HOUSMAN

When I was one-and-twenty

I heard a wise man say,

'Give crowns and pounds and guineas

But not your heart away;

Give pearls away and rubies

But keep your fancy free.'

But I was one-and-twenty,

No use to talk to me.

When I was one-and-twenty

    I heard him say again,

'The heart out of the bosom

    Was never given in vain;

'Tis paid with sighs a plenty

    And sold for endless rue.'

And I am two-and-twenty,

    And oh, 'tis true, 'tis true.

When We Two Parted

LORD BYRON

When we two parted
    In silence and tears,
Half broken-hearted
    To sever for years,
Pale grew thy cheek and cold,
    Colder thy kiss;
Truly that hour foretold
    Sorrow to this.

The dew of the morning
    Sunk chill on my brow —
It felt like the warning
    Of what I feel now.
Thy vows are all broken,
    And light is thy fame;
I hear thy name spoken,
    And share in its shame.

They name thee before me,

    A knell to mine ear;

A shudder comes o'er me —

    Why wert thou so dear?

They know not I knew thee,

    Who knew thee too well: —

Long, long shall I rue thee,

    Too deeply to tell.

In secret we met —

    In silence I grieve,

That thy heart could forget,

    Thy spirit deceive.

If I should meet thee

    After long years,

How should I greet thee?

    With silence and tears.

November 18th, 1845

Monsieur,

I tell you frankly that I have tried . . . to forget you, for the remembering of a person whom one thinks never to see again, and whom, nevertheless, one greatly esteems, frets too much the mind; and when one has suffered the kind of anxiety for a year or two, one is ready to do anything to find peace once more. I have done everything; I have sought occupations; I have denied myself absolutely the pleasure of speaking about you — even to [my sister] Emily; but I have been able to conquer neither my regrets or my impatience. That, indeed, is humiliating — to be unable to control one's own thoughts, to be the slave of a regret, of a memory, the slave of a fixed and dominant idea which lords it over the mind. Why cannot I have just as much friendship for you, as you for me — neither more nor less? Then should I be so tranquil, so free — I could keep silence then for ten years without an effort.

Monsieur, I have a favor to ask of you: when you reply to this letter, speak to me a little of yourself, not of me; for I know that if you speak of me it will be to scold me, and this time I would see your kindly side . . . Tell me, in short, . . . what you will, but tell me something.

I wish I could write write to you more cheerful letters, for when I read this over I find it to be somewhat gloomy — but forgive me, my dear master — do not be irritated at my sadness — according to the words of the Bible: "Out of the fullness of the heart, the mouth speaketh," and truly I find it difficult to be cheerful so long as I think I shall never see you more.

C. B.

Stop All the Clocks . . .
(from Twelve Songs)

W. H. AUDEN

> Stop all the clocks, cut off the telephone,
> Prevent the dog from barking with a juicy bone,
> Silence the pianos and with muffled drum
> Bring out the coffin, let the mourners come.
>
> Let aeroplanes circle moaning overhead
> Scribbling on the sky the message He is Dead,
> Put crêpe bows round the white necks of the public doves,
> Let the traffic policemen wear black cotton gloves.

He was my North, my South, my East and West,

My working week and my Sunday rest,

My noon, my midnight, my talk, my song;

I thought that love would last for ever: I was wrong.

The stars are not wanted now: put out every one;

Pack up the moon and dismantle the sun;

Pour away the ocean and sweep up the wood.

For nothing now can ever come to any good.

When to the Sessions of Sweet Silent Thought

WILLIAM SHAKESPEARE

When to the sessions of sweet silent thought,

    I summon up remembrance of things past,

I sigh the lack of many a thing I sought,

    And with old woes new wail my dear time's waste:

Then can I drown an eye, unused to flow,

    For precious friends hid in death's dateless night,

And weep afresh love's long since cancelled woe,

    And moan the expense of many a vanish'd sight,

Then can I grieve at grievances foregone,

    And heavily from woe to woe tell o'er

The sad account of fore-bemoaned moan,

    Which I new pay as if not paid before.

        But if the while I think on thee, dear friend,

        All losses are restored, and sorrows end.

The First Day

CHRISTINA ROSSETTI

> I wish I could remember the first day,
> First hour, first moment of your meeting me;
> If bright or dim the season, it might be
> Summer or winter for aught I can say.
> So unrecorded did it slip away,
> So blind was I to see and to foresee,
> So dull to mark the budding of my tree
> That would not blossom yet for many a May.
> If only I could recollect it! Such
> A day of days! I let it come and go
> As traceless as a thaw of bygone snow.
> It seemed to mean so little, meant so much!
> If only now I could recall that touch,
> First touch of hand in hand! — Did one but know!

Longing

MATTHEW ARNOLD

Come to me in my dreams, and then
By day I shall be well again.
For then the night will more than pay
The hopeless longing of the day.

Come, as though cam'st a thousand times
A messenger from the radiant climes,
And smile on the new world, and be
As kind to others as to me.

Or, as thou never cam'st in sooth,
Come now, and let me dream it truth.
And part my hair, and kiss my brow,
And say — My love! why sufferest thou?

Come to me in my dreams, and then
By day I shall be well again.
For then the night will more than pay
The hopeless longing of the day.

Coat

VICKI FEAVER

Sometimes I have wanted
to throw you off
like a heavy coat.

Sometimes I have said
you would not let me
breathe or move.

But now that I am free
to choose light clothes
or none at all

I feel the cold
and all the time I think
how warm it used to be.

When You Are Old

WILLIAM BUTLER YEATS

When you are old and gray and full of sleep,
And nodding by the fire, take down this book,
And slowly read, and dream of the soft look
Your eyes had once, and of their shadows deep;

How many loved your moments of glad grace,
And loved your beauty with love false or true,
But one man loved the pilgrim soul in you,
And loved the sorrows of your changing face;

And bending down beside the glowing bars,
Murmur, a little sadly, how love fled
And paced upon the mountains overhead
And hid his face amid a crowd of stars.

What Lips My Lips Have Kissed

EDNA ST. VINCENT MILLAY

What lips my lips have kissed, and where, and why,
I have forgotten, and what arms have lain
Under my head till morning; but the rain
Is full of ghosts tonight, that tap and sigh
Upon the glass and listen for reply,
And in my heart there stirs a quiet pain
For unremembered lads that not again
Will turn to me at midnight with a cry.
Thus in the winter stands the lonely tree,
Nor knows what birds have vanished one by one,
Yet knows its boughs more silent than before:
I cannot say what loves have come and gone;
I only know that summer sang in me
A little while, that in me sings no more.

Love in a Life

ROBERT BROWNING

Room after room,
I hunt the house through
We inhabit together.
Heart, fear nothing, for, heart, thou shalt find her —
Next time, herself! — not the trouble behind her
Left in the curtain, the couch's perfume!
As she brushed it, the cornice-wreath blossomed anew:
Yon looking-glass gleamed at the wave of her feather.

Yet the day wears,
And door succeeds door;
I try the fresh fortune —
Range the wide house from the wing to the centre.
Still the same chance! she goes out as I enter.
Spend my whole day in the quest, — who cares?
But 'tis twilight, you see, — with such suites to explore,
Such closets to search, such alcoves to importune!

Love

PABLO NERUDA

Because of you, in gardens of blossoming flowers I ache
from the perfumes of spring.

I have forgotten your face, I no longer remember
your hands; how did your lips feel on mine?

Because of you, I love the white statues drowsing
in the parks, the white statues that have neither voice nor sight.

I have forgotten your voice, your happy voice; I have
forgotten your eyes.

Like a flower to its perfume, I am bound to my vague
memory of you. I live with pain that is like a wound; if you touch
me, you will do me irreparable harm.

Your caresses enfold me, like climbing vines on melancholy walls.

I have forgotten your love, yet I seem to glimpse you in every window.

Because of you, the heady perfumes of summer pain me; because of you, I again seek out the signs that precipitate desires: shooting stars, falling objects.

I Hid You

MIKLOS RADNOTI

I hid you for a long time
the way a branch hides its
slowly ripening fruit among leaves,
and like a flower of sane ice
on a winter window
you open in my mind.
Now I know what it means
when your hand swoops up to your hair.
In my heart I keep
the small tilt of your ankle too
and I'm amazed by the delicate curve
of your ribs, coldly
like someone who has lived
such breathing miracles.
Still, in my dreams
I often have a hundred arms
and like god in a dream
I hold you in those arms.

I Still Have Everything You Gave Me

NAOMI SHIHAB NYE

It is dusty on the edges.

It is slightly rotten.

I guard it without thinking.

I focus on it once a year
when I shake it out in the wind.

I do not ache.

I would not trade.

Acknowledgments

Permission to reprint copyrighted material is gratefully acknowledged to the following:

Maya Angelou, for "Where We Belong, A Duet," copyright © 1978 by Maya Angelou, from *And Still I Rise* by Maya Angelou. Used by permission of Random House, Inc.

W. H. Auden, for "Stop All the Clocks…," copyright © 1940, 1968 by W. H. Auden, from *Collected Poems* by W. H. Auden. Used by permission of Random House, Inc.

George Bogin, for "Nineteen," copyright © 1972 by George Bogin. Reprinted by permission of Magda Bogin and Nina Bogin.

Rupert Brooke, for excerpted letter, from *Song of Love: The Letters of Rupert Brooke and Noel Olivier*, edited by Pippa Harris, Letters of Rupert Brooke copyright © 1991 by Estate of the Late Rupert Brooke. Letters of Noel Olivier copyright © 1991 by Estate of the Late Noel Olivier. Introduction and notes copyright © 1991 by Pippa Harris. Used by permission of Crown Publishers, a division of Random House, Inc.

Robert Creeley, for "Love Comes Quietly," copyright © 1983 by Robert Creeley, from *Collected Poems of Robert Creeley, 1945-1975*. Used by permission of The Regents of the University of California.

e. e. cummings, for "I carry your heart with me(I carry it in," copyright © 1952, 1988, 1991 by the Trustees for the e. e. cummings Trust, from *Complete Poems: 1904–1962* by e. e. cummings, edited by George J. Firmage. Used by permission of Liveright Publishing Corporation.

Emily Dickinson, for "Heart! We Will Forget Him," reprinted by permission of the publishers and the Trustees of Amherst College from *The Poems of Emily Dickinson*, Thomas H. Johnson, ed., Cambridge, Mass.: The Belknap Press of Harvard University Press, copyright © 1951, 1955, 1979 by the President and Fellows of Harvard College.

97